FUN FACT FILE: ANIMALS!

20 FUN FACTS ABOUT CROCODILES

By Heather Moore Niver

Gareth Stevens
Publishing

Please visit our website, www.garethstevens.com. For a free color catalog of all our high-quality books, call toll free 1-800-542-2595 or fax 1-877-542-2596.

Library of Congress Cataloging-in-Publication Data

Niver, Heather Moore.
20 fun facts about crocodiles / Heather Moore Niver.
   p. cm. — (Fun fact file. Animals!)
Includes index.
ISBN 978-1-4339-6511-1 (pbk.)
ISBN 978-1-4339-6512-8 (6-pack)
ISBN 978-1-4339-6509-8 (library binding)
1. Crocodiles—Miscellanea—Juvenile literature. I. Title. II. Title: Twenty fun facts about crocodiles.
QL666.C925N58 2012
597.98'2—dc23

                              2011023887

First Edition

Published in 2012 by
Gareth Stevens Publishing
111 East 14th Street, Suite 349
New York, NY 10003

Copyright © 2012 Gareth Stevens Publishing

Designer: Michael J. Flynn
Editor: Greg Roza

Photo credits: Cover, pp. 1, 5, 6–7, 8, 9, 10, 11, 12, 13, 14, 15, 16, 17, 18, 20, 21, 22, 23, 24, 27 Shutterstock.com; p. 19 Carol Farneti Foster/Oxford Scientific/Getty Images; p. 26 Justin Sullivan/Getty Images; p. 29 iStockphoto.com.

Printed in the United States of America

CPSIA compliance information: Batch #CW12GS: For further information contact Gareth Stevens, New York, New York at 1-800-542-2595.

Contents

Words in the glossary appear in **bold** type the first time they are used in the text.

Crazy About Crocs!

Crocodiles—or "crocs"—may seem like mysterious beasts. They might seem creepy when they hide silently beneath the water. These **reptiles** are famous for their mighty jaws and sharp teeth. Crocodiles are among the most dangerous animals in the world.

But don't let these characters scare you off. They're awesome animals, even if they aren't the cutest! Did you know that crocodiles are related to dinosaurs? Or that there are 14 different species, or kinds, of crocodile? It's true!

Crocodiles are meat eaters. They use their sharp teeth to catch their food and tear it apart.

Big and Strong

FACT 1

Crocodiles can be longer than a truck.

The dwarf crocodile is the smallest kind of croc. This crocodile is about 6 feet (1.8 m) long. At 20 feet (6 m) long, the estuarine (EHS-chuh-wuh-ryn) crocodile is longer than a truck. And it weighs as much as a car—around 1.5 tons (1.4 mt)!

Crocodiles have a built-in suit of armor.

Croc scales, or scutes, contain bone to make them stronger. Bony plates cover their back. Their powerful jaws have pointed, cone-shaped teeth. Crocs have short legs, but their webbed toes have sharp claws. They also have huge, strong tails.

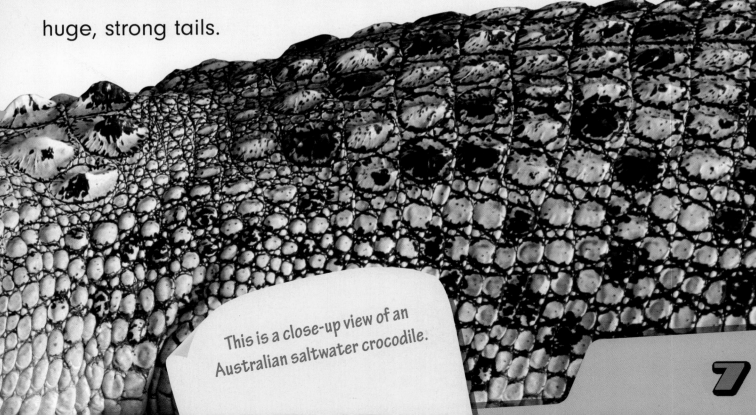

This is a close-up view of an Australian saltwater crocodile.

7

One Big, Happy Family

Crocodiles have been around for about 200 million years.

Crocs, alligators, and other animals like them are called crocodilians (krah-kuh-DIH-lee-uhnz). They first walked Earth at the time of the dinosaurs, but they didn't disappear with the dinosaurs. They **survived**, and they've hardly changed at all since then.

crocodile snout

8

alligator snout

To tell crocs and gators apart, check out their teeth and snouts. Crocs have narrower snouts, and their teeth show even when they're not "smiling"!

Crocodiles are more closely related to birds than to lizards.

Crocodiles look a lot like lizards, and they don't look anything like birds. But appearances can fool you. Crocs and other crocodilians are more closely related to birds than to any other living animal!

Where to Watch for Crocs

FACT 5

Crocodiles are most at home in the water.

Crocodile **habitats** include rivers, swamps, and streams.

Some crocodiles, called "salties," live in salt water. Crocodiles

live in warm or hot areas, such as Asia, Africa, Australia, and the

Americas. They hide underwater with just their eyes showing!

Crocodiles can run 10 miles (16 km) per hour on land.

Crocs like to spend most of their time in the water. But that's not the only place you'll find them. Crocodiles travel on land, too. They can slide on their bellies or walk along with their legs out to the side.

Only a few crocs, such as this African Nile crocodile, can gallop, or run swiftly. Some can run about 10 miles (16 km) per hour!

Crocs to Watch For

Name	Maximum Size	Main Habitat
American crocodile	15 feet (4.6 m)	freshwater and salty coastal waters
Australian freshwater/Johnston's crocodile	10 feet (3 m)	freshwater, often upstream
Cuban crocodile	11.5 feet (3.5 m)	freshwater swamps
dwarf crocodile	6 feet (2 m)	rainforest swamps and slow-moving freshwater
estuarine/saltwater crocodile	20+ feet (6+ m)	all over Asia and the Pacific
Morelet's crocodile	10 feet (3 m)	freshwater areas and some saltwater areas on the coasts
mugger/**marsh** crocodile	16.4 feet (5 m)	freshwater

American crocodile

Philippine crocodile

Name	Maximum Size	Main Habitat
New Guinea crocodile	11.5 feet (3.5 m)	freshwater
Nile crocodile	16.4 feet (5 m)	freshwater and some African coasts
Orinoco crocodile	16.4 feet (5 m)	freshwater
Philippine crocodile	10 feet (3 m)	freshwater areas, like small lakes, swamps, marshes, and branches of large rivers
Siamese crocodile	13 feet (4 m)	freshwater lakes, rivers, and marshes
slender-snouted crocodile	10–13 feet (3–4 m)	mostly freshwater
tomistoma/ Malayan fish crocodile	16.4 feet (5 m)	freshwater

Head of the Class

FACT 7

Crocodiles are very smart.

Crocs aren't just the largest reptile—they're the smartest! They have the most highly developed brains of all reptiles. Crocodiles can learn patterns, such as the times when animals come to the water to drink. They "talk" by growling, grunting, hissing, and roaring.

What's for Dinner?

Crocs can hide underwater for hours.

Crocodiles' eyes, nose, and ears are on top of their head. They can float almost completely underwater for hours as they wait for their next meal to swim or walk by. This is how they surprise their **prey**.

The bumps and flat sides of a crocodile's tail help it speed through the water.

FACT 9

A croc's tail can be as dangerous as its jaws.

Hiding crocs grab land animals when they come to drink. They jump onto land and drag their prey into the water. They drown their prey to kill it. Some even use their strong tails to knock prey into the water.

The Nile crocodile sometimes dines on zebras.

Normally, crocodiles eat small prey such as fish, turtles, and birds. But sometimes they eat bigger animals. Nile crocs are well known for hunting much larger animals. They can easily grab a wildebeest or a zebra and drag it into the water!

Crocs can't chew their food.

Crocs have strong jaws and lots of sharp teeth, but they can't chew! Instead, crocodiles have to tear their food into pieces small enough to swallow. Crocodiles often chomp down on prey and twist in the water to break off pieces.

This crocodile is swallowing a fish whole!

This jaguar in a rainforest in Belize caught a baby croc for lunch.

FACT 12

A croc that misses its prey may become prey itself.

Crocodiles are strong swimmers. They strike with speed. But crocs get tired very easily. If the croc doesn't catch its prey when it first strikes, it may end up being dinner for the animal that it tried to catch!

19

A Crying Crocodile?

Crying crocs aren't really sad.

Have you heard the term "crocodile tears"? It comes from an old story that crocs cry as they eat their prey. But it's not because they're sad. Crocs have body parts close to their throat that keep their eyes wet. When they eat, food presses on those body parts and creates tears!

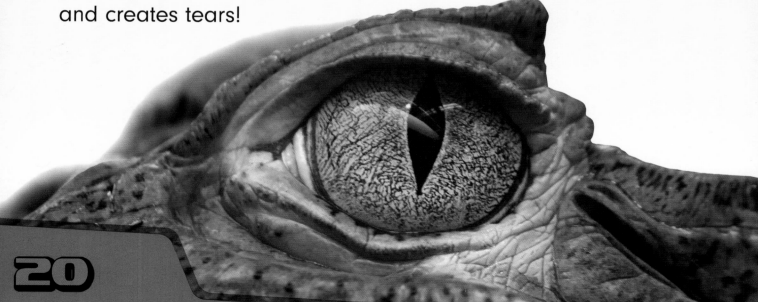

20

Hot Crocs, Cool Crocs

Crocs sometimes sleep with their mouth wide open.

Even a **cold-blooded** crocodile can get too hot. To cool off, a croc might be seen with its mouth wide open as it snoozes. It might simply take a dip in the water, too. Sometimes a crocodile digs a den in the cool mud.

Is this croc sleeping or waiting for its next meal? It's probably best not to ask!

Crocodiles can hold their breath for up to 2 hours.

Temperatures can get too cold for crocodiles. If they can't warm up in the sunshine, they may burrow into mud and sleep. Sometimes they swim to deeper water to relax. If they don't move around too much, crocs can stay underwater for 1 to 2 hours.

Cute Crocs!

Crocodiles may lay up to 90 eggs at a time.

A mother croc may lay between 10 and 90 eggs at one time! Crocodile eggs are about the size of chicken eggs and have a strong white shell. When they're ready to **hatch**, the babies start squeaking. The mother hears them and comes to help them crack their shell.

FACT 17

Mother crocs use their mouths to carry newly hatched babies to water.

Baby crocodiles are only 8 to 10 inches (20 to 25 cm) long at birth. They are prey for birds, fish, and even other crocodiles. Some mother crocodiles carry their babies to water in their mouths or on their backs to keep them safe!

Honoring the Crocodile

FACT 18

Ancient Egyptians honored a crocodile god named Sobek.

Ancient Egyptians kept live crocodiles in temples honoring the god Sobek. In Pakistan, some people still consider the crocodile an honored animal. However, crocs are hunted, too. Their skin is used to make suitcases and shoes. Their **musk** is used in perfumes.

Crocs Rock!

FACT 19

The "Crocodile Hunter" Steve Irwin didn't hunt crocs—he saved them!

Steve Irwin was the star of the television show *The Crocodile Hunter*. As a kid, Steve learned how to jump on crocodiles in the water and wrestle them into a boat! Steve saved crocodiles before they could be hurt or killed someone.

Crocodile Survival

You can "adopt" a croc.

In the last 50 years, about 20 million crocodiles have been killed. People are moving into areas where crocs once lived, leaving the animals fewer places to go. You can make a **donation** to the World Wildlife Fund (WWF) to help protect crocodiles and other **endangered** animals.

Governments have passed special laws to protect crocodiles.

After a While, Crocodile

It's pretty cool that crocs have existed since the time of dinosaurs! Crocodiles make up the largest group of reptiles around today. They're also the biggest and heaviest reptiles.

Some people are afraid of crocodiles. Others honor them. Sometimes crocodiles are hunted to keep people and their pets safe. But too much hunting means that some kinds of crocs are uncommon. We need to protect their habitats and limit hunting if we want to keep crocodiles around for another 200 million years.

Only about 250 Siamese crocodiles still survive in the wild.

29

Glossary

cold-blooded: having a body temperature that's the same as the temperature of the surroundings

donation: a gift of money to a charity

endangered: in danger of dying out

habitat: a place where an animal or plant lives and grows

hatch: to come out of an egg

marsh: an area of soft, wet land

musk: matter from an animal's skin that has a strong odor

prey: an animal hunted by other animals for food

reptile: a cold-blooded animal with scales

survive: to live through something

For More Information

Books

Douglas, Malcolm. *The Crocodile Book: Armoured and Dangerous.* Fitzroy, Victoria, Australia: Black Dog Books, 2009.

Polydoros, Lori. *Crocodiles: On the Hunt.* Mankato, MN: Capstone Press, 2009.

Websites

Crocodile
animal.discovery.com/reptiles/crocodile/
Learn more about crocodiles with games and quizzes, and watch some croc videos.

Crocodiles and Alligators
www.kidsbiology.com/animals-for-children.php?category=Crocodiles%20and %20Alligators
Check out facts and games about all kinds of crocodiles and alligators.

World Wildlife Fund
www.worldwildlife.org
Learn how the WWF helps protect endangered animals and keeps their habitats safe. You can even help out by "adopting" an endangered animal!

Index